Curating Home

CURATING HOME

A Kansas City Poetry Anthology

Poems selected by
José Faus
Marianne Kunkel
Glenn North

Published by Woodneath Press
8900 NE Flintlock Rd.
Kansas City, MO 64157

Publisher's Cataloguing-in-Publication
(Provided by Woodneath Press: A Program of Mid-Continent Public Library)

Curating Home
     p. cm.
ISBN: 978-1-942337-23-2

     I. Poetry / Anthologies (multiple authors)

TABLE OF CONTENTS

Among Kansas City's claims to fame are its fountains, jazz, blues, and barbecue, not to mention the Chiefs and Royals. But the list should also contain its vibrant literary scene, which includes two national literary magazines—*New Letters* and *I-70 Review*—the Midwest Poetry Series, the Riverfront Reading Series, Rose Garden Readings, and The Writers Place, all of which have long supported the city's impressive output of contemporary poetry. *Curating Home* offers a selectifon of work by poets from both sides of the state line. The list, though far from all-inclusive, contains a rich mixture of styles, tones, and subject matter. Don't miss Hadara Bar-Nadav's elegy for her colleague, "When M Becomes a Tree"; Elizabeth Bowman Banks' account of a women who lacks the luxury of choice, "Yellow Daffodils"; Greg Field's youth memoir, "Bone"; Sheri Hall's hymn to her mother (and the source to this anthology's title), "Turned Tables,"; Steve Hatfield's formal ode to his parents, "Bev and Dave"; Hyejung Kook's lament on death of migrant children, "A Summer Day,"; Jenny Molberg's feminist study, "Against the Cult of True Womanhood"; Cameron Morse on a day with his son in COVID time, "Hottest Sports Cars"; Jason Ryberg's hymn to a 39th St. Bar, "Thousand Yard Stare"; Megan Page's meditation on the cost of being gay, "Where Are You From?"; Ann Slegman's portrait of an unloved woman's passing, "Influenza 1883"; Robert Stewart's family memoir, "The Chairs"; and Maryfrances Wagner's tribute to her Italian heritage, "I Am." And don't miss the others, either. Though COVID has curtailed live performances, this anthology should not only help fill that gap but may also introduce you to some poets you haven't read before.

William Trowbridge, Poet Laureate of Missouri, 2012-2016

PREFACE

Curating Home is a collection of poems by Kansas City-metro area poets from both sides of the state line, fully representing poetry throughout Kansas City. Woodneath Press has published it as part of "State of Stories" programming developed by Mid-Continent Public Library's Story Center and the University of Missouri Extension's Community Arts Program. This series of free public programs was created to commemorate the Missouri Bicentennial. As a part of State of Stories, this anthology aims to provide a snapshot of Kansas City at a particular point in time from a variety of perspectives, all expressed in poetic form.

Approximately 300 poems were submitted in July and August 2020 in response to an open call for submissions. The editors, Kansas City-based poets José Faus, Marianne Kunkel, and Glenn North, selected 44 previously unpublished poems by 34 poets. They identified a theme named in Sheri Hall's poem "Turned Tables" that encapsulates the ideas of geography, history, and personal relationships present in many of the poems: Curating Home. Inspired by this theme, local graphic designer Amber Noll created the book cover. The final product is an anthology of Kansas City poetry, with a theme provided by a Kansas City poet, and cover art created by a Kansas City artist.

Essentially homegrown, this anthology stems from the Story Center's mission to provide services that help people create stories, share those stories, and connect with the stories of others. Woodneath Press, the publishing imprint of the Story Center and Mid-Continent Public Library, is a key way that the Story Center achieves its mission. This anthology fits squarely with the Press's commitment to publishing "local authors, local content."

Without the dedicated efforts of many, even a relatively modest project like this would not be possible. In particular, we want to thank the editors—José Faus, Marianne Kunkel, and Glenn North—for their thorough readings and thoughtful discussions; William Trowbridge for his concise foreword; Amber Noll for her perfect representation of the anthology's theme; the William T. Kemper Foundation—Commerce Bank, Trustee, for its financial support; and, especially, the poets who have provided us with new opportunities to appreciate and think about the lives and places in Kansas City at this, for many reasons, historic time.

Dave Burns, Story Center Publication Manager
Mark Livengood, Story Center Director
Kansas City, March 2021

BABA YAGA BOUGHT THE HOUSE ALREADY LIKE THAT
OR I THOUGHT THIS WOULD BE DIFFERENT
    Erin Adair-Hodges

The forest offered few options.
This thicket hulks so black

    sunlight's a rumor among mushrooms.

Everything quivers its little prayer
with not enough gods to hear.

    I hear. Poppy seeds

shriek from the soil to be seen,
to be known

    as the mortar wants the plunge

of the pestle. I'd nursed other plans,
sent instead on missions by maybe mothers

    for fire and into the fire.

To marry, to mother a little death.
There was something else

    I'd meant to do with that broom.

You enter the woods one way
but are not the same when you leave it.

    If you leave it.

Listen—what is a house but a thing that waits,
married to the earth. Waiting gnarls a bone.

    This house—it wants to run.

HOST
    Erin Adair-Hodges

Welcome to my good home it is made   from lightning and anise

inside is enough room   for you   and up to

one-third of all your   disappointments

the spare room has been lent   to a week in May of 1991—

Havishamish, it likes   keeping to itself, hush

your happiness when you   walk by

feel free to use the pillows   the hundreds of pillows

in Colorado the papers are black   with the pillow shortage

but we are ok   here I think sometimes of giving half

and some nights all   away

I am not brave in that way   or what way

One thing is stay away   from what would seem to be

a linen closet, what with   it being small and in the hall—

it has turned into   *Waldeinsamkeit,* a forest

loneliness, and I am   afraid not of

losing you to it but   losing it to you

THE INCORPORATED TOWN OF FARLEY
    Shannon Ashley

The sign still reads *Population 269*, but I know
people have died, more have been born.
My sister contributed four to the growth;
although one was lost to divorce. For years,
her tears were the flood waters that wore away
the old, copper green bridge. I always drove
down the middle, so the edges wouldn't crumble
under my tires. They replaced it with freshly
cemented blocks the year I left, so I would know
I could never come home again.

The bank, once residence of my mother's career
and my first job shredding paper, has cleared
of tellers and cash, filled by excommunicated priests
of St. Pius X in need of an office. Their cloister remains
hidden by back road anonymity and trees. But I see it.
My mother prayed for their souls, their return to *the right
path* when we power-walked past one summer evening.

The Lutheran church, which I rarely entered
but whose sign hid my first kiss with the pastor's
son, has taken away my golden lit memories of gravel
and grass, turned them to concrete. The shouts
of pirates sailing the air in a ship shaped tree
house have been replaced by cars and prayers.

New houses line roads which were once empty hills
of mist at sunrise. The trained pigeons kept by Claude,
the original owner, finally all flew away. The mercantile
is a music shop which never opened for business.

Yellow Daffodils
　　Elizabeth Bowman Banks

Dedicated to the countless women who never had the luxury of choice.
And for Cousin Minnie, who told me her story.

Four tiny graves for the ones
we couldn't afford to keep.
Cans of turpentine, blue tansy, long
knitting needles. I know if I do it quickly
the pain isn't as bad, but oh God--
the blood, you never get used
to the blood. Staining my dress, the
sheets, pooled on the kitchen floor
the color of red summer cock's
combs, my dirty bare feet reflected in
the shiny surface.

The sooner it can be done the better
off I'll be, don't wait too late or John
will be able to tell from my swelling
belly and he'll complain about how we'll
feed them, we both know we can't.
I'll tell him I have my monthly,
he'll lay off for a few days while I
wait for the pain deep in my belly
to cease. I'll do it quickly,
while the kids are at school,
the baby is sleeping, and John
is gone, down the road working
Turkeys, his clothes smelling like
bird shit, feathers caked on the soles
of his patched work boots.

I dig the holes behind the whitewashed house
large enough to place the carefully wrapped
handkerchief--mint green, blue, pink, once
a pretty lace. Cover it with soil, and
when he asks I'll tell him the little mound of new
dirt will be yellow spring daffodils.

NOW IS THE TIME
    Hadara Bar-Nadav

Mary said, *Now is the time
to get well,* a phrase that tries
to nod its bobble head
with encouragement
but falls flat in a pool
of drool. I used to agree to
agree to such things: *Get well.
Okay!* Go to sleep now,
little cancerous thought.
Go to bed now, death-
obsessed girl. Better yet,
gulp your meds and join
your joyful friends as you
Disney through your days,
solving the latest plague
in a six-minute news show.
Sexual dysfunction: solved
by a thirty-second commercial
during *Modern Family* reruns
and a little blue pill. Never
mind the four-hour erection
that may require a hospital
stay. A broken heart?
There's a new dating app
for that. Finally, we can
stop trying since time will
heal all wounds. Just wait
for the next commercial
break for the *newest, best,
guaranteed or your money-
back tip* for total oblivion.
Then lie down with me under
the kitchen table where
a clump of dust looks like
a baby bunny we can claim
as our own and a recluse
spider knits our names
in the stars. Soon we will
get better-than-ever together.

WHEN M BECOMES A TREE
    Hadara Bar-Nadav

M. texted the word *bliss* three times
before she died. Her last intelligible word.
She was being eaten from the inside.

Her lungs, bones, lymph nodes. Her brain.
Tumors raiding her language and memory,
uncentering her centers, so all she had was *bliss*.

The forests were on fire, and this was bliss.
Her husband and daughter cried
at her bedside, and this was also bliss,

and the dog refused to leave her room bliss.
Even with an oxygen machine breathing
for her bliss and her vast list of opioids bliss.

Paralyzed in a bed in her living room bliss
where she could see her beloved dogwood
bliss loss of speech bliss moaning bliss

up and out into the petalled softness of a tree.

anyway. It's so overrated.
You've received two shots
of morphine and won't shit
for two days, but who cares.
Go hug your IV. What's worse
is the dead man's vertebra
grafted into your neck.
Scaffold for your cervical
spine, you living puzzle,
you polyamorous paradox—
rodded, screwed, then zipped
back up. Now your whining
and tears conjoin with a dearly
departed who is trying to help
you hold up your own skull.
Don't you want to know his
toy poodle's name or that
he had 13 sexual partners
and none of them ever kissed
his neck like the palomino
he longed to be? I wouldn't kiss
your neck now either. You smell
like Lysol, canned peaches,
and lemon-scented death.
Your moaning makes me
moan. Your moan is not
your own. If I yell again
at the nurses they'll call
security. They'll call god
and tell her to take me back.
Take me back, or give me
that next shot of morphine
instead—its silver weight
like cool mercury eeling
under my skin. Who wants
to feel anything else? Who
wants to feel at all? No one
dies in this poem. So there,
I've blown the suspense.
We just go on living from
one pain to the next, begging
a bored nurse for mercy.

COMING UPON A PAINTING FOR MY DAD
AT THE NELSON-ATKINS MUSEUM
    Phyllis Becker

"I, too, stand on the edge of it with a prayer lamp."
—Noah Davis

Dad's back is to us.
We hunger to see more of him.
His shoulders are slightly rounded, head bowed.
He stands in the cavity of a cave
in his dad jeans and slightly large polo.
The insides of the cave's brown rocky walls
forms a U-shape, and above, below, and around him is the universe.
The backs of his dark brown arms and afro
are outlined by the light of the *prayer lamp* he holds.
He's on the verge of stepping off.
He is blackness and stars.

GUIDE TO THE FLINT HILLS
    Susan Carman

The gravel road will slow you
    to a measured pace
as you wend
        your way
through green-covered drifts
    of limestone and chert.

Big bluestem rules
  this sea of grass,
      but behind a checkering
of barbed wire, sprays
  of gayfeather, penstemon
and Indian paintbrush flaunt
  their colors.   Watch

red-tailed hawks
    swerve and coast
        on downward drafts.
Listen for sputtering
    horses or cattle lowing
        in a nearby pasture.

See how clouds cluster
  on the horizon like mountains,
      seaming earth to sky.
You'll feel small
  among these windswept swells,
      and so you are—but you fit.

Linger on a ridge,
    step into the waves of grass.
Let the vastness
      of this ancient ocean
    wash over you
with the wind
        your only witness.

Another Invitation
    Malcolm Cook

By the still bend of another slow river
at the outskirts of another hard town
the railway bridge gives morning shelter
from last evening's horizontal storms.
Its graffitied trestle testifies
to the high school's wins and losses.
To the midnight bravado of its young lovers,
who surely swooned and pet beneath the rattling rails.

Chill morning's sharp and sudden gust
of cattail fluff from muddy flats below.
A creosote tinge of ancient sunken barge.
Black campfire coffee. Startled birds swerve in flight.
Departing, a line of cottonwood. A lone colt braces.
Empties hurled from pickups blaring country music.
The long-haul semi driver interrupts the naked pavement,
at least until the interchange with highway thirty-five.

Well past the furthest edge of town,
with dusty drive, a clapboard house
greets strangers with a red tin cup
hung from a sun-scorched metal chain.
The screaking ancient water pump
runs clear & cold from frigid depth.

Then, offers of sliced cheese on bread,
and room enough to pitch a tent.
No questions asked. Lies to defend.
A simple honest hand extended.

Piñon and sage drift from behind
a freshly painted garden shed.
A stacked stone fence gives telltale sign
of work and hearth and sleep and sweat.
A single taut suspended line
brings news of birth and sudden death.

Bone

    Greg Field

My mother worried how far into the woods I'd go,
how far along the quiet road I'd walk.
She did not bother praying. She hung the wash
on lines near the grapes and opposite the plums.
She figured Buddha and the Great Father
would keep an eye out. Blood was spilled,
bones cracked regularly, and bread burned.
There were no rules, scars grew like odd flowers
across the tilled hills. Coyotes gathered to cry
and complain till they reached the far sheds,
where evenings, my father drank and remembered
morning hunts. The sun illuminated the grainy
wood floor between our beds. After school, I went
in search of bones, wandering the woods,
pastures, and wading the creek, feeling with toes.
A cracked cow's skull sliced my foot open—
the water billowed red as I dug it from the mud.

Mᴜ Nᴜ
    Jack Granath

It hangs there, Hung   Liu's large-scale painting,
two women toiling   in a river.
A tow rope of   some kind connects them,
that and the river   and their gender
and the title: *Mother and Daughter*.
They bend, their fingers   almost touching
water and rock.   The artist likes
to let a little   linseed oil
run down from top   to bottom edges
overnight and wreck   the false perfection
of the finished   work, so runnels
rivulet   their way across
the figures,   mirroring their tears
and rain and time,   the violence—
especially the violence   of time.

Imagine a   Madonna, the
mighty child   protected in
the manger of   her arms, or think
of Mary Cassatt,   Picasso, Klimt,
or anything   with warm, pink skin,
and stable, centered   composition.
Here the center gapes,   a void,
the figures drudging   at the edges,
bound to each other   but separated,
tied to their load   but moving forward,
if only on the wet,   bare feet of time.

One day,
as gods count days,
the Missouri River
just up and changed its course.
Native tribes who lived
along its banks recited the story.
Mothers chanted to daughters,
fathers lectured sons
about the heaving earth,
how it lifted the water into the sky,
and offered it to the sun.
When the light rejected the gift,
tribal ancestors
compelled giant snakes
to carry the water
through a maze of twists
and turns across the prairie
to fill a wandering hollow.
The river, in its flight,
forgot to hide from white settlers
who thanked their Lord
for the rich river soil
waiting for their plows.

Hand painted china
red rose pattern,
Mahogany piano
next to three-legged screw-top stool,
Horse-hair divan
tightly woven, tufted ebony cushion,
Golden oak table top
sits askew on hand-turned pedestal
center leaf missing,
Small mound of stones, placed with loving care

TRAFFIC JAM
    Sheri Hall

The traffic in this city is horrid
Especially on a Saturday morning
        Swerve to dodge pot holes
        Frustrated
        Over stimulated
        Honking horn
        Flashing lights
        Why they tryna swerve 'round me
        Like I'm just sittin' here for my health
        As if there ain't a LONG LINE of cars in front of me
        Whose lights are on
Someone went home…Is always going home

Every Saturday morning
A homegoing celebration makes the hood cry
        Black asphalt
Under a cloud of depression
        Making the city streets
        Wanna disappear so much they hide
        Under a blanket of cars
        Parked on sides of streets
        Wrapped blocking side streets
        Parking lots hold vehicles
As they hold each other
Needing consoling during this time of bereavement

Every night furrow browed sages
And politician lips ignite with judgment
        Young girls need to close they legs
        Boys need to pull up they pants
        But saggin' pants ain't caused these traffic issues
        Your generation did … Handed down a curse
        You expect us to fix with a belted waist line
        Buckles and knocked knees
        Won't be a sign stopping bleed on concrete
        Cases stay open longer than caskets
        Killers kick it at vigils carrying candles
Flickering flames as if their rage weren't a whole damn forest fire

Burning family trees
Leave seedlings
>*It stays hot in these streets*
>*Match light to kindling*
>*Spreading cross kin folk*
>*Ain't no throne in this game*
>*Winter ain't coming*
>*Yet people are still dying*
>*We shower in tears*
Flooding the land with grief
>*Pretending that mustangs regulate traffic*
But everyone knows 5.0s aint trustworthy in the rain

Most times they spin out of control
Causing more harm
>*They can't Disjoin*
>*This slow rush hour*
>*Blocking the highway*
>*Rolling gun battle through the processional*
>*Shots pop off at the funeral*
>*Only the weak*
>*Tryna pull up at a burial*
>*Drive by brought us all together*
>*Dripping exhaust*
Exhausted from them same heels sinking in that same mud

Weak after weeks of peeps in these roads tripping
Tail pipe dreams extinguished from another young someone
>*Future gone up in smoke that no one wanted*
>*Because no one never wants this smoke*
>*Or the next smoke*
>*Smoked ham at the repast*
>*Leaves a memorable taste alongside*
>*The spaghetti red prophecy*
>*Someone else finna get they noodle peeled*
>*Leave sauce splatter memorabilia on a slab*
>*They fresh meat meeting they maker*
Soon enough a bullet will kiss the cook

>*The cycle continues another young one roasted*

I stare at the plate with anxiety
Over stimulated by an abundance of family
> These newfound cousins and
> People are nice and all
> But I'm irritated, ready to leave
> I don't move a muscle tho
> I stay, help clean the kitchen
> I sit back down
> Because to leave means
> I'm back in traffic
> And I'm tired of seeing so much traffic
It's traumatic

Momma taught me: *preservation*,

How to care for Muh'Dear,
How to keep ancestors in harmony,
How to band and conduct the score,
The art of keeping home.

Pillows fluffed and blood wiped up.
Sweat cleaned and crumbs removed.
Evaporated tears in the sacred Corners of her pristine.

Keep her close, never discard.
No nursing home. No landfill rot.
Never give her away for someone Else's wares. Treasure her.

Momma taught me *reverence*.

I find: comfort in Muh'Dear's
Lap; smells of joy and working hands.
I sit placing my arm on hers,
Held like the little girl I once was.

Her skin whispers a familiar, familial Melody; a combo of blues and
swing.
Culture soaked tapestry, and flyness On warm light flooded walls.

Her record spinning a sound of
Jim Crow survival, big band, number Running, Bible thumping,
Moonshining, funk ballads and trap.

A symphony orchestrated classically
Combining sounds old and new;
Constructed for lasting wisdom,
Speaking the tune of the ages.

Momma's generation found a way to
Scratch tables without ruining legacy; Marks a revolving break beat. Her
Heart beat's in the breakdown.

Momma taught me *love*

With skilled scratch and smooth horn
While cleaning. Muh'Dear taught History on wooden floors furnishing
The house holding descendants.

We own. We kept. We keep. We Care. We pass down. We inherit.
We no longer own our hip-hop or Jazz, but we own these artifacts.

We retain these spirit filled things. She holds the groceries then we use
Her recipes. Eat in the good chair as
She watches over us secured on high.

We protect her. We protect Blackness, African Americana. We
Protect them from the hands that Seek to steal, destroy, appropriate.

Momma taught me: *concealment*,

How to trick them,
How to hide and protect our history,
How to keep a vault of exhibits,
The art of curating home

A Few Houses Down from Thor's
    Steve Hatfield

Can someone blessed as I complain? I mean,
Of course my life is good. I work, I play,
I love; the woman keeps the castle clean
(Or clean enough), and everyday
I get a power nap. It's just, it's all
So meh, so beige. Just once I'd like to see
Some color in my life I can't recall
Encountering before. An enemy
In red, perhaps, a blackguard, battle-scarred,
Who'll meet me on the lea— I'd flip his grin
Then dare the dandelions in the yard
To flaunt their yellow gloves at me again.
They are my glory's bane, those smirking weeds—
I kill and kill and kill, but nothing *bleeds*.

My father fabricated steel
For thirty deafening years,
Then set a trailer at the lake
Without applause or cheers.

My mother did a housewife's work
Then built a business up
That netted them that double-wide
But not the winner's cup.

If either ever dreamed of fame,
Those dreams today are laughs;
They did what life gave them to do
And signed no autographs.

Tonight a crappie fry sounds good;
They'll watch Mom's favorite show.
Before the obits note their deaths,
What else is there to know?

GIMMEE ALL THAT JAZZ
    Robert Hill

gimme all that jazz
        gimme hand-slapping toe-tapping
gimme butt-bumping shoulder-slumping hambone
        gimme hives of jive to bumble in
gimme Coltrane
        gimme tons of sweet-and-sour saxophonic gumbo
gimme sacks of Satchmo
        gimme steel-eyed blood-soaked hot-sweating virtuosos
(but dont gimme any of those old cotton fields back home)

gimme babies wrapped in swaddling clothes of blues
        gimme salvation in the key of G
gimme firefly conventions on sweltering July nights
        gimme screen-porched old men,
gimme store-front church and Yes Lord Yes
        gimme miles of aisles of hat-passing hope
gimme riffs of raw confession
        gimme sanguine sass for the least of these
(but dont gimme any of that sitting at the back of the bus)

gimme daily gumption and nightly bliss
    gimme fortitude in the face of all temptation
gimme volcanic cool and blizzardy fire
    gimme hope on the hurricaned tornadoed conflagrated road
gimme enough so we dont ever take no money that says we aint fit to walk
the earth
    gimme peace in the valley of dry bones
gimme time, straight 4/4 time and lilting 3/4 time at the same time
    gimme one more second even when there aint any more time
(but dont gimme any of that pretending im invisible)

gimme Benny and Count and Jay and Tim and Ida
        gimme Bird wrapped in linens of grace
gimme Ella resplendent in bolts of pure lightening
        gimme Big Joe and your clear-eyed atonement
gimme the languor of your purest scatting sorrow

  gimme the jubilee of your cross-eyed reconciliation
gimme the dagger of your worst goodbye
   gimme the smile in your best hello
(but dont gimme any of that jazz unless your gonna gimme all of it)

FIRST ANNIVERSARY IN KANSAS CITY
    Marcia Hurlow

You want to love what I love.
As we watch the dawn parade
of street cleaners, slow and heavy

as a military convoy, your eyes rove
to the detritus floating in the road.
You want to love what I love

and in this moment, that is fragments
of shiny metal and maple tree seeds
that street cleaners move as slowly

as this July morning that hovers
at the open window next to our bed.
You want to love what I love

so here you are, your broad hands
hold the white curtains from the sill
and the dust of street cleaners, heavy

with summer grime. Later we will work,
still later, walk along together
through the clean streets, slowly
talk about what we both will love.

STREET CARS
    Silvia Kofler

There once was one called *Desire,*
Kansas City enjoyed them
fifty years ago
until Detroit carmakers
made them disappear.
Some tracks are still
left over in old Westport.
Now, we've got a new line,
all 2.2 miles of it.
Its streetcars are sleeker
and quieter than fifty years ago.
However, some car accustomed drivers
haven't learned to park
within the white lines
and a Benz took a beating.
A lady stopped on its
tracks motions the conductor to
drive around her car.
After fifty years it takes some
getting used to.

A Summer Day
    Hyejung Kook

The kids are playing in the backyard pool, my son, 6, in the shallow end,
diving for little hoops, my daughter, 4, holding onto the steps,
blowing bubbles and kicking, both covered head to toe,
sunscreen in white streaks across their faces and ears and necks,
soft and skinny, the brownest part of them despite the many applications,

and I marvel that such a slender thing can hold up their heavy heads.

In anatomical drawing, the ideal figure has a head to body ratio
of 1 to 8, but a toddlers' is about 1 to 5, and now I am thinking
of my son as a newborn, my fear that if I didn't support his head
just right, hand gripping gently yet firmly against the base of his skull,
his neck might snap. I know now that little ones are tougher

than I thought that my child can fall out of a shopping cart headfirst

onto concrete and be fine, that a child can sleep uninterrupted
after a possible concussion, that their fevers run high, that brain damage
doesn't occur until reaching 108 degrees Fahrenheit,
but I also know that drowning doesn't look like drowning,
a drowning person cannot wave their arms but instead extends them

laterally, pressing down, their mouth bobbing in and out of the water

as they struggle to breathe. I know that it takes a single unguarded moment
for a child to slip beneath the surface, beyond notice. I can't help
but recall the image of Alan Kurdi, his little toddler body lying face down
at the beach, as if asleep, his wet red shirt rucked up above his waist,
and seeing it, I wanted to pull it down and cover the soft skin of his belly,

the way I do for my sleeping children because a bare tummy might make
them sick.

I know that immigrants and asylum seekers are dying in and shortly after
detention,
like Mariee Juárez, not even 2 years old, who caught a respiratory
infection
at a center in Texas and ran a fever of over 104 degrees—when my own
child's

fever passed 104, despite cool compresses and dosing with acetaminophen
and ibuprofen,
we stripped down for skin to skin, which can help regulate body
temperature,

and I felt like a mad thing rocking my child, feeling that limp body burn
like a brand

between my breasts for hours before the fever finally broke—
but Mariee grew sicker, and after release from detention, she died
in a hospital from viral pneumonitis. We can't know if she'd have lived
if she hadn't been detained, but we do know her mother Yazmin sent her
daughter's body, alone, back to Guatemala to be buried with her relatives.

I know thousands of detainees have tested positive for COVID-19.

I know children who arrived without a parent or legal guardian
have been held at Fort Sill, home to the Army's main artillery school,
now designated as an emergency shelter, once a Japanese internment
camp,
or more precisely, as Lawson Fusao Inada writes, described by
"the War Relocation Authority" as "camps" or "centers" for:

"Assembly/Concentration,/Detention,/Evacuation,/Internment,/Relocation,
—/among others"

and earlier still, the place Geronimo and the other Chiracahua Apache
were held 20 years in violation of their terms of surrender, and here I am
sitting in the shade of a magnolia, watching my children scream in delight,
not drowning, the sun gleaming on the water and their upturned faces,
the August heat a benediction rather than a scourge, and I wonder,

what more should I be doing with this one life?

할머니 / HALMONI
    Hyejung Kook

How is it I don't know your name?

How is it I know that as a child   during the occupation

you had your name taken away
              were given a Japanese one

but I still don't know your name?

I think of my parents

every day during pandemic   but do not call.

Why is so much left unsaid?
           So much left unasked?

What stone is in my mouth?

When I was a child

Grandmother   we went back to Korea

when you still lived by the sea.
          When I scraped my forearm

you licked your finger

rubbed saliva into the wound.

I recoiled in disgust.   You called it 약 (yahk).

But I didn't understand.
         I asked my father

why you called it medicine

and he said that when you have lived without

you manage with   whatever you have.

The day we walked
                              Daechon Beach together

I saw bladderwrack tossed up on the sand

and the bumps revolted me.

I didn't know then   certain seaweed can't survive

without vesicles
                        air-filled bladders lifting

their sinuous brown lengths up to the sun.

I didn't know extracellular vesicles

in saliva   help blood to clot

and so does promote healing.
                              This morning I finally call

my parents and learn your death anniversary was yesterday.

Three years you've been gone.

Let the mouth   do its work unconstrained.

In a sea of grief
                        I learn to breathe underwater

that your name is 윤정임.

THE LITTLE CREEK
    Patricia Lawson

It was a now and then, off and on little creek
that ran in its little valley at the bottom of the street.
It dried up in summer, but in wet weather rose
high enough to flood a basement.
In spring it drew us, and we flowed it into the woods,
especially when the sweet Williams and the May apples blossomed.
Once, hoping to catch a water bug, we scooped
its muddy waters into a clear jar and watched the water
separate into muck below and clear brown above.
And surprise! we found a round brown water boatman,
who swam around just for us, then hid in the muck.
The next day we released him and wondered
if he and his fellow boatmen followed
the meandering creek south through the woods
into someone else's bigger creek,
and on and on into the Kaw, the Missouri
and the big wide waters of the world.

AGAINST THE CULT OF TRUE WOMANHOOD
  Jenny Molberg

"They are only semi-women, mental hermaphrodites..."
—Henry F. Harrington, of Suffragettes, the *Ladies' Companion*, 1838

"It is not the custom to employ females!" the man
of the story exclaims like a broken parrot.
Kate Warne, 23, America's first female detective.
Kate my talisman as I drive to court to face my abuser
for the third time. It's 1856. Or it's 2019. Kate foxes
her way into high secessionist society, dressed
as a fine Southern lady, champagne flute an appendage,
fleur-de-lis pin glinting with impending war. The men flirt
with their gold-plated pistols. Kate's eye stenographs
the folds of a flag, the violining of fly legs on a corpse,
the slave-trader's side-eye behind his canteen.
Enigma Kate, AKA Kitty Warren, Kay Warner, Mrs. Barley,
Mrs. Cherry—even her gravestone misspelled: WARN.
A mayday. Kate, a reminder that even a woman
who saves the President must shut up.

*

On a train from Harrisburg to Baltimore, Kate Warne
dresses Abraham Lincoln in a shawl, a soft felt cap,
and he poses as an invalid while she never sleeps,
her blue eye an invisible searchlight. She plays
rich woman, Mrs. Secessionist, purveyor of all things
ruined with charm. Sometimes I take a plane
to go to court, sometimes I drive. This goes on
for months, the judge's dismissal, the man's appeal,
my poems shoved in the hands of lawyers, a judge
lowering her glasses, a judge shaking her head, a judge
finding the better language with which to excuse me.
The man says I killed his baby. I'd never been pregnant.
The man's face purples on the bench. I speak of how
I hid for three years, forcing my shaking hands between my thighs,
how I was afraid to sleep or bathe. I must submit
even to the destruction of my own body. Now on the train
the Western front is quiet. Stars like splatters of luminol
against the sky's black floor. The judges have finally
purged my record, my poems tucked back in a book.

But when the silence rumbles, thuds of a man's footsteps
throb down the hallway, and when I lower my spyglass,
a stain darkens my clothes.

32

BUTTERFLY WEED
    Jenny Molberg

They derange themselves across the yard
in ecstatic blaze so the monarchs will come
on their way to the high mountains, where fir trees
morph into giant cones of breathing glass.
I stab the rusted shovel in the spot beside the window
the day we decide we will never have children.
The shovel belonged to a man who used to hurt me.
Turning the black clay over, I have severed
several pink worms into segments that writhe.

THE MYSTIC LOSES HER WAY
Diane Mora

They said it would happen. Life
Would return to the point
Where it would become harder to find
The secrets of eternity
In piles of dirty laundry and stacks
Of dirty dishes.

They said it would happen. Dust
Bunnies would stop leaving clues
To the universe in their tracks.
Stained clothes, soiled pots and pans,
Would be just that.
Nothing more.

No more mysteries left in them.
As if all they had to tell
Had finally washed off and slipped quietly
Down the drain with
The rinse water.

Hottest Sports Cars
    Cameron Morse

Theo and I hike the hillside in June sun to the soccer fields outside James
Lewis Elementary, the playgrounds of Pink Hill Park festooned with
yellow tape, the abandoned school utterly still. Only my boy and I stir
here, tracing the brick-and-mortar contours of the gymnasium into recesses
of black glass that reflect back to us our feral selves: my shaggy temples,
his naptime hair an exploded bird's nest. I try a door handle. Demonstrate
the lockdown for my two-year-old. Theo forages a lost golf ball.
Desperation hit, days earlier, when one of his Montessori classmate's
mother tested positive, and what other choice for us but to work for the
living we have and hope for the best? Out in bright windy light, I hear the
clink of lanyard to the silver mast of the flagless pole. Theo gathers gravel
from a rock bed for his imaginary dump truck. Downhill from the Walker
Family Cemetery, a hilltop copse for the dead shelterers of outlaw Jesse
James, we unfold our first library book since the start of the pandemic,
delivered through the window of my Toyota Sienna by a masked librarian,
and enter the pantheon of Ferrari, Lamborghini, Porsche.

Leaving
    Cameron Morse

I haven't
shaved my head or trimmed
my beard in weeks. For five years,
you have placed me here
in this dying orchard, a shag
of stickers, leafy shoots
trying to branch from a gloomy
bough. Sparrows chitter
and here they come again, house
sparrows chatting at the foot
of the driveway. Theirs is a life
as unpaid for, as undeserved
as my own. Grandma fills the feeder,
dashes leaf rot from the bird bath.
I rest my left arm encased in fiberglass,
swaddled in co-bind. Measure
time until the next dose of Norco.
Like Velcro straps we cleave
to the places we're born in, we're born
again in, the trees we plant:
eastern redbud, Japanese maple,
serviceberry. Even the magnolia
that doesn't make it leaves with a fistful
of the earth it was bound to. Children
learn the names we teach them and say them
better than we do. Five years ago,
You placed me in the flight path of endless
pink petals. You lifted me into the gurney
and gave me someplace to rest.

Where Are You From?
    Megan Page

I am from talks with my mother in the car.
Road trips to funerals in small towns
Before I knew what death was.
In the background, Bob Dylan
Introduces me to poetry.

I am from my father not telling me he loved me
When I told him I am gay.
And the text he later sent.
And the late nights on leather sofas
With tears streaming down my mother's face.

I am from chasing fireflies on summer evenings.
The caterpillar I discovered on a camping trip when I was six,
I watched her turn into a moth.
And then die.
My mother never understood why this made me sob.

I am from fear of doctors and germs and uncertainty.
The nights I thought I couldn't breathe because I watched the whooping
cough PSA
Before my cartoons.
Pertussis sounds like the name of a greek goddess.
If only she didn't kill children.

I am from Sunday school worship songs.
Churches where questions weren't welcome.
Writing messy prayers to messier gods
Asking them to answer, to help me, to grant me understanding.
I'm still asking.

I am from soil and saying I love you when I didn't mean it.
But that wasn't the question you were asking, was it?
You are filling the time, the space between us
Because these moments of not knowing what to say
When the world is loud,
These moments are where you're from.

WHAT TO LOOK FOR
    Trish Reeves

Pale lime green is one way to say it,
or maybe lilac, also pale, or vivid
green the color of light to fill the window
and mirror as I settle my eyes
and think, The falling out
lasts and lasts, yet every year
about this time, I'm on good terms
with a world so cruel
kindness makes me weep.

THOUSAND YARD STARE
    Jason Ryberg

an ode to D.B. Cooper's bar, 39th street, KC/MO

It was a hole-in-the-wall kind of place
that stank of Pinesol, piss and stale beer,
and still had dispensers in the men's room
for glow in the dark condoms and French ticklers
and other *surprise novelty items*,

and the big monkey behind the bar was named
Earl or Jake or Curly and he kept a sawed-off
table leg within reach at all times and gave you
that thousand-yard-stare if you dared ask
for anything with more than one ingredient,

and the jukebox hadn't been changed-out
in decades and the *lunch special* was always
the same: *pickled eggs, pork rinds and hot sauce,*
though I got the feeling that nobody
ever ate it unless they lost a bet.

LANE ENDS. MERGE LEFT.
    Cecilia Savala

Ordinary life: oil change
for a haircut. You left only

Ordinary days: pink pencil in my hair,
drug references, images of

Ordinary advice: like
when you reserve your seat—

on a Saturday, a coupon—
four ice cubes in the tray
in the shape of an L.

I think in lines—
helicopter blades beating the wind
bathing in recycled dinosaur bones.

pull all the way up to the service doors,
call one minute after the hour.
Nobody puts ketchup on a hot dog.

ALL THE WEST SIDE GIRLS LOVE LOU DIAMOND PHILLIPS
    Lauren Scharhag

Summer of '88 and *La Bamba*
was released on VHS.
Us West Side kids
had found our idol.

Before that, we got excited
whenever Speedy Gonzalez
appeared on our TV screens.
There was an old Chevy Chase
film my mother loved mostly
for the sassy Mexican cook
with whom she shared a name,
Aurora, and we loved anything
with Cheech Marin. If there were
other bits of Mexico in pop culture
at the time, I'm hard-pressed
to think of them. (Desi Arnez
was Cuban. Also: black-and-white.
No, thank you.) But we held them
to our hearts like talismans.

Mexicans were still exotic back then
in the way that Italians were exotic
in 1905. My friends didn't know
what a tamal was. When they came
to dinner, they tried to eat it
husk and all. The only Mexican restaurants
in town served tacos in store-bought shells,
and everything came with a side
of refried bean puree, smothered
in white cheese that was like a mockery
of queso fresco. But suddenly,
everyone knew the song, "La Bamba."
They played it everywhere,
at the supermarket, at school dances,
and even the white girls agreed,
Lou Diamond Phillips was so cute.

He wasn't even Latino,
but we loved him anyway.

My tío made bootleg copies
for everyone and we watched it
over and over. We knew
all the songs, every dance move.
We re-enacted them on the front porch,
using a broom as a guitar, a hairbrush
as a microphone. We were amazed
that someone could sing in Spanish
and sound cool, none of the warbling ballads
or cheesy corridos heavy on the accordion
that we knew from our abuela's records.

We girls started wearing our hair
in high, 1950s ponytails, tied with big bows.
Our Catholic school saddle oxfords
were suddenly stylish. The boys either
combed their hair into pompadours
or wanted black leather jackets
like Bob. Now, thirty years later,
my cousin still thinks he's Esai Morales,
roaring around on his motorcycle,
and I can't hear "Sleep Walk"
without getting choked up.

Stand and Deliver came out
that same year, but a math teacher
isn't nearly as sexy, and we had to wait
ten years for *Selena,* for Jennifer Lopez
to come with her nalgas and spangled bras.
(Also not an actual Mexican,
but we'll take what we can get.)

INFLUENZA 1883
     Ann Slegman

The locket around her neck
held a tintype of the infant
she lost to fever. Her bed
was a dark stain of dampness,
her limbs a loose skein of yarn.
No milk-sweet mouth to nurse,
no soaked diapers to change,
the smooth hand-made cradle
removed to the barn. She thought
she loved her husband, but now
that she was empty, a brittle
husk, he paced the small rooms,
night after night chewing on tough
stews, that it would be soon, all
too soon, the slow, last gasp, the sheet
over her face, the ping of dirt
on the lowered coffin as he searched
the crowd of mourners for yet another
farmer's daughter, soft as a corn silk,
to share his bed.

Unpleasant facts are what it feels like to be crowded by nothing but you.
Unpleasant facts seem less about the snowcover, less about what was
there before the snow came down, everything about the melted wash
merge of the thereafter. Unpleasant facts say what we will look like
in twenty-five years. Unpleasant facts play constantly in their own
shadows. Unpleasant facts salt the imagination before drowning it.
Unpleasant facts begin as glitter and end with a blowtorch. Unpleasant
facts catch in the throat in the long moment before they're believed.
Unpleasant facts usually steer clear of most sexual encounters, returning
to highways, hospitals, and nations under threat. Unpleasant facts refer
to you as seagull mouth and afterimage with a bang. Unpleasant facts
are not the name for unpleasant facts. Unpleasant facts don't care.

THE CHAIRS
    Robert Stewart

The technician placed the chairs
on a sheet of glass when I challenged
the evenness of the legs, there

in the back room where he had
stored them for pick up.
He said the floor was uneven,

but so what? I wanted chairs
that sit solidly on any surface,
a Roman road or side street,

as I know women in a village
in Sicily take their wooden chairs
to the street to visit with friends,

or when I was a kid, our folks would
carry the steel-tubed kitchen chairs
with vinyl seats into the backyard,

where my aunts and girl cousins,
and very own dad, in fresh overalls,
and my Uncle Joe, God bless him,

and the McCarthys next door,
God knows who else, were dragging
lawn chairs and stools, getting

the dog to move, and forming
a circle in the evening, solid
as my great aunt Sanina, sitting

on the wooden bench, her legs
beneath a flowered dress spread,
which is how I imagine she

steadied herself for the crossing
from Palermo to Naples to New York,
Chicago and down to St. Louis.

So I ordered these four, solid-teak
chairs when I got my own place,
and I wanted them not to move.

I AM
    Maryfrances Wagner

I'm from red sauce, garlic, and fig trees,
mantiglie, wine barrels, and Frank's Jewelry.
My zie told stories, grew basil, made cannoli.
My Nonno loved *O Solo Mio,* Da Vinci, La Cappella Sistina.
I'm from calamari, carciofi, Scimeca's salsiccia,
Sunday pasta, Christmas sphingi, homemade anisette,
from Maria and Antonio, Bessie and Frank, Salvatore
and Marguerite. I'm from *si mangia, vieni qui,*
and *ciao,* Nonna's calloused knees and rosaries.
I'm from Kansas City, Palermo, Bivona, and Florence,
the sea and the mountains, goats and herbs, Zio Nene's
grin, Nonna's gardenias, Nanno's mandolin. I'm from
floors you can eat on, stiff towels dried on lines, sinks
scrubbed to a perfect shine. I'm from homemade
ricotta, glistening olive oil, late-night wakes, tatted lace,
bread boards passed down, the ship Germania, from roots
without soil, the one left standing, waiting for a place.

ODE TO A MALE SEAHORSE
    Maryfrances Wagner

Fins, monkey tail, chameleon eyes,
you're no horse. Your limber
tail can scratch your head,

drape your neck, or hang
on seaweed like a crochet hook
while you vacuum plankton

and tiny shrimp—until your life-long
mate begins the seductive dance.
Together you swirl, blush,

tuck heads, twine tails, flirt,
chirp, hum, snap. Nose to
nose, you form a sea heart.

She drops eggs in your pouch
and wanders off to fatten up.
You tend the nursery. You sleep

in wide-eyed dormancy,
orange in coral,
yellow in sponge.

The day fry swarm in a stream
of apostrophes, hundreds,
all at once, swirl up

and vanish. Little time
to doze among mangroves
before she returns,

all hums and snaps.

VIGIL
   Lindsey Weishar

Lumen Christi Monastery, Kansas City, KS

Moon, a bright eye tooth,
night, a freckling of stars.
Sidewalks overgrown, glittered
with glass.

Glass beads catch street lamps,
as the Little Brothers and Sisters
lead us by candlelight across
busy streets long past

their signal, through darkened
neighborhoods, where figures
have gathered on porches
and in the streets

to listen to Hail Marys
that alternate English and Spanish.
Up the road, the red, white,
and blue pulse

of police. Two nights ago
on 10th Street, four people died
in a bar by bullet. Tonight,
the Sisters and Brothers pray

through a microphone, repeating
Scripture, repeating, "Wounded,
I will never cease to love,"
into unlighted streets,

fingering the joyful mysteries
of a rosary caught like a kite
in the trees. Can there ever be
joy again, light

when it leaves the eyes
of a beloved? The Sisters
and Brothers hand their neighbors
candles—a homeless man,

a woman and her young daughter—
baptism of wax and flame.
Not all will be dark. The chill
of the evening seeps

through the seams of our clothes
at a grotto with a painting of Maria
in bright red. Under her,
a small, leafless tree.

In its branches, a red cardinal.
The prayers return dark to its
silence here. Candles return
night to its stars.

Grace & Holy Trinity Cathedral
Ruth Williams

The old woman was speaking not to me, but
at me, her mouth unfurled, ferns of white

in her hair. Her husband dead, the house they bought
far from the city, her friend, the poet,
shaky with Parkinson's, her own voice wavering,
she couldn't sing the Easter arias this year,

so she'd stayed in the nave and gestured along
to the choir's resurrection, a tune she knew by heart.

While she spoke, I noticed a candle flickering
and I imagined each of her words was a wind

in my eye's iris, like the wavering of the world's
light at the birth of Jesus Christ.
Each digressive points was a stone
hinging open, slowly, oh, so slowly

until it cracked open, a savior in the glitter
of the inner seams. This was my faith statement,

listening, the act I laid at Jesus' feet,
though I no longer profess belief.
Still, even I understood her mouth
was a sacrament, a moth caught
in the upper registers of the cathedral, flying
without pattern, only faith.

MISSOURI
    Ruth Williams

Soft smell of smoke,
the continual return of wind
from up river. Churning
of bodies at the water's edge,
the same couple clasped
two days in a row. I take
a cyclical pleasure
in remembering yesterday
how she waited for him to let go first,
attuned to his need. Today,
I want to let my hips
assert themselves
with a similar kindness.
The blue bowls of darker dirt
along the shore's shelf scatter
to make room for the driftwood's
long, white bone. Alone,
every man I pass
becomes a talisman
I hold tight
in my line of sight, wishing
for the river to come
through those two,
pressed like lips,
to kiss each blue note
along my shore.

Drowning
        Tina Yochum-Magaz

Froilan Magaz of Leon, Spain
Smashes stone with a pick ax,
Grinds away his self-esteem.

Arrives America, 1918, via Mexico:
Revolution, terror,
Decaying bodies lying
In the streets.

Manager,
Of a German thread factory,
To breaker of stones.
He leaves his pride behind
In Mexico,
With tangling,
Trailing spools
Of colorful thread.

Looks through a streaked window,
Curses raindrops
On workdays.
No wages in hand.
Four hungry children,
Mexican wife,
Sixteen years his junior.
Prays for work, sunshine,
Warmer days.

Froilan's will,
Tenacious as granite
Endures,
While breaking,
Missouri stone.

Heavy boulders shatter,
His dreams,
Falling away like chips of limestone
As he swings the ax
And sings
Spanish operas
In this strange,
New land.

A Berlin Fairytale in Haunted Times
    Amy Zoellers

I'll take two hours of heavy smoking
and moderate drinking in a seedy bar with
post-punk industrial musician Mr. Bargeld.
We will wallow, how we'll wallow
until the whisky makes his eyes droop and the
smoke-haze between us nearly walls us in,
Nat King Cole on the jukebox
doing leftover Christmas numbers in English.
If we are unable to think of anything to wallow about,
we'll make something up.
Outside the rain will pour.
I'll wear a black turtleneck and blue lipstick
and pink Lucite elephant earrings intended for
my niece's birthday, though the joke would vault
right on over her smartypants
clean-living
high-school head.
Herr Bargeld will be wearing his bouncing explosion of
1983 post-punk hair whether he likes it or not.
Colored lights blink upon a pitiful Christmas branch.
The gin is marvelous. Let's make it a pink one this time.
To match my earrings.
My niece's earrings.
In the New Year I vow to quit swearing,
to write two songs a month,
as well as a series of breakfast-themed villanelles.
And to floss regularly, once and for all.

José Faus is a visual artist, writer, performer and independent teacher/mentor with an interest in the role of artists as creative catalysts for community building. He is a founder of the Latino Writers Collective and sits on the boards of The Latino Writers Collective and Charlotte Street Foundation. His writing appears in numerous anthologies. His chapbook *This Town Like That* was released by Spartan Press. His second book of poetry *The Life and Times of Jose Calderon* was published by West 39 Press.

Marianne Kunkel is the author of *Hillary, Made Up* (Stephen F. Austin State University Press) and *The Laughing Game* (Finishing Line Press), as well as poems that have appeared in *The Missouri Review*, *The Notre Dame Review*, *Hayden's Ferry Review*, *Rattle,* and elsewhere. She is an Associate Professor of English at Missouri Western State University, where she directs the creative writing program. She holds an MFA in poetry from the University of Florida and a Ph.D. in English from the University of Nebraska-Lincoln where she served as the managing editor of *Prairie Schooner* and the African Poetry Book Fund. She currently is the editor-in-chief of Missouri Western State University's national literary journal, *The Mochila Review,* and advisor of its campus literary journal, *Reach.*

Glenn North is currently the Executive Director of the Bruce R. Watkins Cultural Heritage Center. He holds an MFA in Creative Writing from UMKC. Glenn is the author of *City of Song,* a collection of poems inspired by Kansas City's rich jazz tradition and the triumphs and tragedies of the African American experience. He is a Cave Canem fellow, a Callaloo creative writing fellow and a recipient of the Charlotte Street Generative Performing Artist Award. His work has appeared in numerous journals such as *The Langston Hughes Review*, *The African American Review,* and the *American Studies Journal.* He collaborated with legendary jazz musician, Bobby Watson, on the critically acclaimed recording project, *Check Cashing Day* and is currently filling his appointment as the Poet Laureate of the 18th & Vine Historic Jazz District.